To the past and future children

of the movement.

JANUARY 20, 2009.

WHEN MY PARENTS FOUND OUT I'D BEEN **ARRESTED** AND GONE TO JAIL, THEY WERE DEVASTATED. I WAS AN EMBARRASSMENT, A SOURCE OF HUMILIATION AND GOSSIP.

SO I STOPPED COMING HOME AS MUCH.

I STILL SAW MY FAMILY OVER THE SUMMER AND ON BREAKS HERE AND THERE, BUT **NASHVILLE**--AND THE GROWING NASHVILLE STUDENT MOVEMENT--

--BECAME MY **HOME**.

MARCH: BOOK TWO

WRITTEN BY JOHN LEWIS & ANDREW AYDIN
ART BY NATE POWELL

NASHVILLE, TN--
NOVEMBER 10, 1960

HAMBURGERS
TAKE ALONG A SACK FULL

EXCUSE US,
MA'AM--?

USING NONVIOLENT SIT-INS,
OUR YOUNG ORGANIZATION HAD
SUCCESSFULLY **ENDED** SEGREGATION
AT THE LUNCH COUNTERS DOWNTOWN.
NEXT, WE TURNED OUR ATTENTION
TO **FAST FOOD RESTAURANTS**
AND **CAFETERIAS**, USING THE
SAME STRATEGY.

BY RESPECTFULLY INSISTING TO BE TREATED FAIRLY, WE WOULD DRAW ATTENTION TO THE **UNFAIRNESS** OF SEGREGATION.

YES WE'RE OPEN

MA'AM--

may we be served, please?

I WAS BEGINNING MY SENIOR YEAR AT AMERICAN BAPTIST, AND ANY TIME NOT DEVOTED TO MY SCHOOL WORK WAS SPENT PLANNING, PREPARING, AND ORGANIZING.

FALL 1960 WAS MARKED BY A CONTENTIOUS PRESIDENTIAL ELECTION CAMPAIGN BETWEEN VICE-PRESIDENT RICHARD NIXON AND SENATOR JOHN F. KENNEDY.

KENNEDY NARROWLY WON.

BRITE-O

BRITE

WHAT THAT WOULD MEAN FOR ME-- AND FOR AFRICAN-AMERICANS IN GENERAL-- I DID NOT KNOW.

FUMP

BUT OVERALL, I WAS OPTIMISTIC.

IT WAS A FUMIGATOR.

USED ONLY FOR KILLING PESTS.

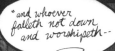

"and whoever falleth not down and worshipeth--

AT FIRST, I DIDN'T BELIEVE THAT MAN COULD'VE REALLY LEFT US THERE TO DIE.

"shall the same hour be cast into the midst of a burning fiery furnace--"

WERE WE NOT **HUMAN** TO HIM?

NOW SHOWING
CECIL B DEMILLE'S
: TEN COMMANDM::NTS

FEBRUARY 1961 -- NASHVILLE, TN.

one for THE TEN COMMANDMENTS, please.

BUT AS THE VIOLENCE GOT WORSE, OUR PROTESTS BECAME MORE AGGRESSIVE.

CAN I HAVE ONE TICKET FOR THE TEN COMMANDMENTS, PLEASE?

I'M SORRY -- I CAN'T SELL YOU A TICKET.

WE BEGAN HOLDING "STAND-INS" AT LOCAL SEGREGATED MOVIE THEATERS.

THE TACTIC WAS BORROWED FROM STUDENTS AT THE UNIVERSITY OF TEXAS IN AUSTIN.

hi -- I'D LIKE ONE FOR THE TEN COMMANDMENTS.

SORRY -- CAN'T SELL YOU A TICKET.

next.

WHEN THEY REFUSED US, WE WOULD GET BACK IN LINE AND WAIT OUR TURN TO ASK AGAIN.

HUP TWO THREE FOUR

HUP TWO THREE FOUR

FOR MORE THAN TWO WEEKS,

WE PROTESTED EVERY NIGHT.

AT FIRST,

IT WAS JUST THE LOCAL WHITE TEENAGERS WE HAD TO WORRY ABOUT.

IN RESPONSE TO THE ESCALATING VIOLENCE, THE CENTRAL COMMITTEE HELD A MEETING THAT INCLUDED ALLIES LIKE **REV. WILL CAMPBELL.**

LOOK, THE VIOLENCE **IS** GOING TO GET WORSE AND WORSE UNTIL SOMEONE IS KILLED--

HOW CAN IT BE THE RIGHT THING TO DO, TO CONTINUE PUTTING YOUNG PEOPLE IN HARM'S WAY?

WHAT DO **YOU** THINK, JOHN?

BUT I HEARD NOTHING THAT NIGHT TO CHANGE MY MIND.

uh huh,

I RESPECTED CAMPBELL AND THOSE WHO SHARED HIS CONCERNS,

we're gonna MARCH.

--AND WHAT DO YOU THINK WE SHOULD DO ABOUT THE **POLICE,** WHO ARE JUST AS DANGEROUS AS SOME OF THE OTHERS?

we're gonna MARCH.

SO THE NEXT EVENING, I LED THE PROTESTS.

KLIK

NOW SHOWING
CECIL B DEMILLE'S
THE TEN COMMANDMENTS

BUT THERE WAS NO VIOLENCE.

TWENTY-SIX OF US WERE ARRESTED.

EVEN THOUGH I WAS SUPPOSED TO GIVE MY SENIOR SERMON THE NEXT DAY,

you know the drill-- whites to the left, coloreds over here!

WE REFUSED TO POST BAIL.

SO I SPENT FEBRUARY 21, 1961 -- MY TWENTY-FIRST BIRTHDAY -- IN JAIL.

U.S. CAPITOL -- 10:21 AM, JANUARY 20, 2009

NOW ENTERING
MURFREESBORO,
TENNESSEE

almost there!

LEWIS, YOU BE **CAREFUL.**

I KNOW YOU'RE STARTING THIS JOURNEY IN WASHINGTON, BUT AFTER YOU GET GOING, WELL-- THESE PLACES ARE **NOT** LIKE NASHVILLE.

YOU'RE HEADED INTO THE **DEEP SOUTH--** THE HEART OF THE BEAST.

I KNOW, BUT THIS IS SOMETHING I **HAVE** TO **DO.**

JOHN, I LOVE YOU, BROTHER-- KEEP YOUR **EYES** ON THE **PRIZE.**

I'LL SEE YOU AGAIN IN A FEW WEEKS, BERNARD.

one way or another.

IN LATE MARCH 1961, A FRIEND SHOWED ME AN AD IN **THE STUDENT VOICE,** A MONTHLY SNCC PUBLICATION.

29

IT ANNOUNCED THAT THE **CONGRESS OF RACIAL EQUALITY (CORE)** WAS SEEKING VOLUNTEERS TO TEST THE SUPREME COURT DECISION FROM THE PREVIOUS YEAR, **BOYNTON V. VIRGINIA**,

DC, huh? okay, back of the bus.

WHICH OUTLAWED SEGREGATION AND RACIAL DISCRIMINATION ON BUSES AND IN BUS TERMINALS.

ITS TITLE WAS SIMPLE.

FREEDOM RIDE 1961

ACTUALLY, BERNARD AND I HAD WRITTEN A LETTER EARLIER THAT YEAR TO **REV. FRED SHUTTLESWORTH,** TALKING ABOUT AN IDEA WE HAD FOR A SMALL GROUP OF INTEGRATED STUDENTS TO RIDE BUSES INTO BIRMINGHAM TO TEST THE **BOYNTON** DECISION.

HE WROTE US BACK, BUT SAID HE THOUGHT IT WAS TOO DANGEROUS, AND THE SITUATION IN BIRMINGHAM TOO **VOLATILE.**

YOU ARE NOW LEAVING

SO WHEN I SAW THAT AD, I FELT IT WAS THE **SPIRIT OF HISTORY** AT WORK AGAIN.

ON MY APPLICATION, I WROTE: "I KNOW THAT AN EDUCATION IS IMPORTANT AND I HOPE TO GET ONE, BUT HUMAN **DIGNITY** IS THE MOST IMPORTANT THING IN MY LIFE.

"THIS IS THE MOST IMPORTANT DECISION IN MY LIFE— TO DECIDE TO GIVE UP **ALL** IF NECESSARY FOR THE FREEDOM RIDE, THAT JUSTICE AND FREEDOM MIGHT COME TO THE DEEP SOUTH."

THEY LET ME IN.

APRIL 30, 1961.

LOOKING OUT AT **WASHINGTON, DC** FOR THE FIRST TIME IN MY LIFE WAS **MAGICAL**.

I HEADED TO **THE FELLOWSHIP HOUSE**, WHICH WAS RUN BY QUAKERS AS A SORT OF HEADQUARTERS FOR PACIFIST ORGANIZATIONS.

NOK NOK

KLIK

JOHN, WELCOME--

JIM PECK -- HE HAD BEEN ON CORE'S FIRST FREEDOM RIDE, THE JOURNEY OF RECONCILIATION IN 1947, WHICH LANDED ALL ITS PARTICIPANTS IN A CHAIN GANG.

ELTON COX -- A MINISTER FROM NORTH CAROLINA.

DR. WALTER BERGMAN, A PROFESSOR FROM THE UNIVERSITY OF MICHIGAN, AND HIS WIFE FRANCES.

THERE WAS JIMMY McDONALD -- A PLAYFUL GUY, HE WAS A FOLK SINGER FROM NEW YORK.

18-YEAR-OLD CHARLES PERSON, A PHYSICS STUDENT FROM MOREHOUSE COLLEGE.

ED BLANKENHEIM -- CORE STAFF MEMBER.

GENEVIEVE HUGHES -- A CORE FIELD SECRETARY.

THERE WAS ALBERT BIGELOW -- A PACIFIST ARRESTED IN 1958 FOR STEERING A SKIFF CALLED THE GOLDEN RULE INTO A NUCLEAR TESTING ZONE IN THE SOUTH PACIFIC, PROTESTING THE USE OF ATOMIC WEAPONS.

HANK THOMAS -- A HOWARD UNIVERSITY SENIOR.

AND JAMES FARMER -- THE LEADER OF OUR GROUP.

TOGETHER, WE SPENT THE NEXT THREE DAYS TRAINING, PREPARING OURSELVES FOR WHAT LAY AHEAD.

WE BEGAN BY COVERING MUCH OF WHAT I HAD SPENT YEARS LEARNING FROM JIM LAWSON-- **GANDHI, THOREAU, EMERSON**...

WE LEARNED LOCAL AND STATE LAWS. LAWYERS LECTURED US ON OUR RIGHTS UNDER THE **BOYNTON** DECISION, AND WHAT COULD BE DONE IF THOSE RIGHTS WERE **DENIED**.

THERE WAS VERY LITTLE DOWNTIME, BUT ONCE OR TWICE JIMMY McDONALD PICKED UP HIS GUITAR AND SANG.

which side are you on, boy--? ♪ which side are you on? ♪

ON THE NIGHT BEFORE WE STARTED OUR JOURNEY, WE WENT OUT TO EAT AT A NICE CHINESE RESTAURANT.

I HAD NEVER ACTUALLY **EATEN** AT A RESTAURANT BEFORE IN MY LIFE--

THE ONLY OTHER TIMES I HAD STEPPED FOOT INSIDE ONE HAD BEEN PART OF A **PROTEST**.

CLINK CLINK

≡ ahem ≡

IF I COULD GET YOUR ATTENTION, PLEASE--

HE MAILED COPIES TO PRESIDENT KENNEDY,
ATTORNEY GENERAL ROBERT F. KENNEDY,
FBI DIRECTOR J. EDGAR HOOVER, TO THE
CHAIRMAN OF THE INTERSTATE COMMERCE
COMMISSION, AND TO THE PRESIDENTS OF BOTH
GREYHOUND AND TRAILWAYS BUS COMPANIES.

THOSE LETTERS WERE
NEVER ANSWERED.

OUR FIRST STOP WAS FREDERICKSBURG.

LOOKS LIKE THEY KNEW WE WERE COMING AND BAKED US A CAKE.

IT WAS THE SAME IN RICHMOND AND PETERSBURG, WHERE WE STAYED THE NIGHT.

WE LEFT THE NEXT MORNING FOR FARMVILLE, THEN ON TO LYNCHBURG AND DANVILLE.

IN CHARLOTTE, JOE PERKINS ASKED FOR A SHOESHINE IN A BARBER SHOP, AND WAS PROMPTLY ARRESTED FOR TRESPASSING.

JOE'S CHARGE WAS THROWN OUT THE NEXT DAY, BUT BY THEN WE WERE IN ROCK HILL, SOUTH CAROLINA.

I COULD TELL WE WERE IN TROUBLE AS SOON AS I STEPPED OFF THE BUS.

WHITES

THAT NIGHT WE STAYED AT FRIENDSHIP JUNIOR COLLEGE, AND ALMOST AS SOON AS I GOT THERE,

I RECEIVED A TELEGRAM.

IT WAS FROM THE AMERICAN FRIENDS SERVICE COMMITTEE-- THE QUAKERS. THEY'D TRACKED ME DOWN THROUGH NASHVILLE--

THEY WERE INVITING ME TO COME TO PHILADELPHIA FOR A PHYSICAL, AND TO COMPLETE MY INTERVIEW FOR A TWO-YEAR VOLUNTEER PROGRAM IN **INDIA** THAT WAS VERY SIMILAR TO THE PEACE CORPS.

IT WAS A TOUGH DECISION--
I'D OFTEN IMAGINED LIVING ABROAD.

SO I DECIDED TO GO
TO PHILADELPHIA.

IF ALL WENT AS PLANNED, I'D
TAKE A FLIGHT BACK TO NASHVILLE
AFTER MY INTERVIEW, AND THEN
TAKE A CAR TO BIRMINGHAM ON
SUNDAY, MAY 14ᵗʰ-- MOTHER'S DAY--
TO **REJOIN** THE FREEDOM RIDERS.

BUT MY GROUP NEVER MADE IT
TO BIRMINGHAM.

WEDNESDAY, MAY 17, 1961-- BIRMINGHAM CITY LIMITS.

TEN OF US SET OUT FROM NASHVILLE TO TAKE THE PLACE OF THE BLOODIED RIDERS WHOSE BUSES WERE ATTACKED IN ANNISTON AND BIRMINGHAM, AND TO PICK UP WHERE THEY LEFT OFF.

BUT THE **POLICE** CAUGHT UP TO US BEFORE WE MADE IT ALL THE WAY INTO TOWN.

YOU TWO--

STAND UP

YOU'RE UNDER ARREST FOR VIOLATING STATE LAW--

YOU **KNOW** WHITE PEOPLE AND NIGGERS CAN'T SIT TOGETHER!

JIM ZWERG AND **PAUL BROOKS** WERE TAKEN TO JAIL ALMOST IMMEDIATELY.

WE WERE ALL ON EDGE, KNOWING WHAT THIS CITY HAD DONE TO THE **OTHER** RIDERS.

EVERYONE ELSE--

PLEASE PRODUCE YOUR TICKETS.

DR. BERGMAN, STILL BLOODY FROM THE FIRST BUS'S ATTACK IN ANNISTON, WAS BRUTALLY BEATEN AGAIN ON THE TERMINAL FLOOR IN BIRMINGHAM.

≡ ahem ≡

HE SUSTAINED PERMANENT BRAIN DAMAGE AND A STROKE THAT WOULD **PARALYZE** HIM FOR THE REST OF HIS LIFE.

59

THEY WERE BRAVE AND COURAGEOUS PEOPLE TO TAKE US ALL IN.

WE STARTED DOWN THE HIGHWAY AND HEARD A NEWS BULLETIN:

THIS JUST IN--THE FREEDOM RIDERS ARE BACK IN NASHVILLE, AND HAVE RETURNED TO THEIR COLLEGE CAMPUSES...

WE WERE ECSTATIC THAT THEY DIDN'T KNOW WHERE WE WERE--

BUT THE MOOD QUICKLY FADED.

THEY-- WE ARE NOW REPORTING THAT THE STUDENTS ARE ON THEIR WAY TO BIRMINGHAM IN A PRIVATE CAR.

wha--!

hang on, everybody--

THEY KNEW WE WERE COMING.

time for a DETOUR!

SOMEHOW, WE MADE IT BACK UNDETECTED THROUGH LESS-TRAVELED ROADS.

WE ALL HAD A MEAL TOGETHER BEFORE BEING DRIVEN DOWN TO THE GREYHOUND STATION TO RESUME THE FREEDOM RIDES.

FINALLY, WE WERE ALLOWED TO GO INTO THE SO-CALLED WHITE WAITING ROOM, WHERE WE STAYED THE ENTIRE EVENING.

WE WERE HEARING A **LOT** OF THINGS AT THE TIME, BUT DIDN'T KNOW WHAT TO BELIEVE.

WHITE ONLY

--AND WE HEARD THAT BOBBY KENNEDY SAID, "THE PEOPLE HAVE A RIGHT TO TRAVEL"--

but he wants all of you OUT of Birmingham.

He thinks Birmingham is too dangerous.

ALL I KNEW WAS THAT ATTORNEY GENERAL ROBERT KENNEDY COULD NOT COUNT ON **ANY** COOPERATION FROM STATE OR LOCAL AUTHORITIES.

WHITE ONLY

WE HEARD THAT ROBERT KENNEDY AND HIS AIDE, **JOHN SEIGENTHALER**, HAD BEEN TALKING TO GOVERNOR **JOHN PATTERSON** AS WELL AS GREYHOUND OFFICIALS TO WORK OUT A SOLUTION.

KLAK KLAK KLAK KLAK KLAK

WHITE ONLY

WE HAVE A BUS READY.

I know, and I don't care.

I know.

Joe, please.

I'M SUPPOSED TO DRIVE THIS BUS TO DOTHAN, ALABAMA, THROUGH MONTGOMERY, BUT I UNDERSTAND THERE'S A BIG CONVOY DOWN THE ROAD.

I ONLY HAVE ONE LIFE TO GIVE, AND I'M **NOT** GOING TO GIVE IT TO **CORE** OR THE NAACP.

IT MAY SOUND STRANGE, BUT AT THE TIME I WAS MORE SHOCKED THAT THIS WHITE BUS DRIVER KNEW ENOUGH ABOUT US TO REFERENCE **CORE** BY NAME.

PEOPLE WERE STARTING TO NOTICE US, EVEN IF WE DIDN'T CHANGE THEIR MINDS.

EVERYTHING WAS UP IN THE AIR UNTIL BULL CONNOR SHOWED UP TO TALK TO THE DRIVER, ALONG WITH GREYHOUND OFFICIALS AND LEADERS FROM THE LOCAL BUS DRIVERS' UNION.

FINALLY, AT 8:30 IN THE MORNING ON MAY 20, 1961, WE RESUMED THE FREEDOM RIDES.

I-65 SOUTHBOUND, 5 MILES OUTSIDE
MONTGOMERY, AL--
9:55 AM, MAY 20, 1961.

FIRST BAPTIST CHURCH--
MONTGOMERY, AL-- 8:08 PM, MAY 21, 1961

S-S-BOOM!

AFTER HEARING OF THE VIOLENCE AT THE
BUS STATION, DR. MARTIN LUTHER KING, JR.
FLEW TO MONTGOMERY.

A MASS MEETING WAS CALLED
AT RALPH ABERNATHY'S CHURCH.
GOVERNOR PATTERSON, DESPITE PROMISING
TO PROTECT US, HAD WARRANTS SWORN
OUT FOR OUR ARREST. WE RIDERS
DECIDED TO SCATTER OURSELVES
THROUGHOUT THE CHURCH'S PEWS IN
CASE THE POLICE TRIED TO ARREST US.

all right!

yeahh!!

BOOM!

BURN IT!

so now... let's clean these niggers outta here!

CREAK F-BOOM!!

BY SUNSET, MORE THAN 1,500 PEOPLE HAD PACKED THE CHURCH.

JUST AS THE CROWD INSIDE THE CHURCH
GREW, SO DID THE CROWD OF WHITES
OUTSIDE. AND THEY WERE ANGRY.

83

THE MEETING DIDN'T BEGIN UNTIL FRED SHUTTLESWORTH ARRIVED SAFELY WITH JAMES FARMER.

DR. KING INTRODUCED FARMER TO THE CONGREGATION, AND BROUGHT HIM UP TO THE PULPIT.

THEN THEY ASKED ME TO COME UP AS WELL.

THE TWO REMAINING ORIGINAL FREEDOM RIDERS-- REUNITED.

AS THE MEETING CONTINUED, WE POURED OUR HEARTS INTO THE MUSIC OF THE MOVEMENT, SONGS LIKE "AIN'T NOBODY GONNA TURN ME 'ROUND" AND "WE SHALL OVERCOME", TO GIVE US STRENGTH.

TINK!

CRASH!

SMASH!

T-TINK TINK

CRASH!

MEANWHILE, AS I SOON LEARNED, DR. KING HEADED TO THE OFFICE FOR A PHONE CALL WITH ROBERT KENNEDY.

I WAS ASKED TO JOIN JAMES FARMER AND DIANE NASH AS DR. KING EXPLAINED ROBERT KENNEDY'S REQUEST.

I WON'T STOP IT NOW. IF I DO, WE'LL JUST GET WORDS AND PROMISES.

IT IS NOT WITHOUT MERIT TO SAY THAT THE FREEDOM RIDE HAS ALREADY MADE ITS POINT, AND NOW SHOULD BE CALLED OFF.

NO.

THE NASHVILLE STUDENT MOVEMENT WANTS TO GO ON. WE CAN'T STOP IT NOW, RIGHT AFTER WE'VE BEEN CLOBBERED!

PLEASE TELL THE ATTORNEY GENERAL THAT WE'VE BEEN COOLING OFF FOR 350 YEARS--

IF WE COOL OFF ANY MORE, WE WILL BE IN A DEEP FREEZE.

THE FREEDOM RIDE WILL GO ON.

very well.

I'll tell him.

UNEXPECTEDLY, THE ALABAMA NATIONAL GUARD ARRIVED AND SENT THE MARSHALS AWAY.

AFTER HOURS OF REFUSING TO SPEAK WITH ANY FEDERAL OFFICIAL, GOVERNOR PATTERSON HAD FINALLY ORDERED MONTGOMERY TO BE PUT UNDER WHAT HE CALLED "QUALIFIED MARTIAL LAW."

AND SO, WE CONTINUED OUR MEETING.

WYATT WALKER SPOKE, FOLLOWED BY RALPH ABERNATHY, AND THEN JAMES FARMER. BUT DR. KING BROUGHT IT HOME.

GOVERNOR PATTERSON BEARS THE ULTIMATE RESPONSIBILITY FOR THE HIDEOUS ACTION IN ALABAMA.

HIS CONSISTENT PREACHING OF DEFIANCE OF THE LAW, HIS VITRIOLIC PUBLIC PRONOUNCEMENTS, AND HIS IRRESPONSIBLE ACTIONS HAVE CREATED THE ATMOSPHERE IN WHICH VIOLENCE COULD THRIVE.

THEN FRED SHUTTLESWORTH SPOKE, AND MADE IT QUITE PLAIN.

IT'S A SIN AND A SHAME BEFORE GOD THAT THESE PEOPLE WHO GOVERN US WOULD LET THINGS COME TO SUCH A SAD STATE. BUT GOD IS NOT DEAD.

THE MOST GUILTY MAN IN THIS STATE TONIGHT IS GOVERNOR PATTERSON.

FINALLY, JUST AFTER MIDNIGHT, THE MEETING FINISHED.

WE STARTED TO LEAVE,

ONLY TO FIND THAT THOSE SAME TROOPS SUPPOSEDLY SENT TO PROTECT US, NOW **HELD** US INSIDE THE CHURCH.

OUT OF THE WAY--

ALL RIGHT, BACK UP, **BACK UP!**

GENERAL HENRY GRAHAM OF THE ALABAMA NATIONAL GUARD,

A REAL ESTATE AGENT IN HIS CIVILIAN LIFE,

REFUSED TO ALLOW ANYONE TO LEAVE.

KLOP

KLOP

STOMP

:ahem:

"WHEREAS, AS A RESULT OF OUTSIDE AGITATORS COMING INTO ALABAMA TO VIOLATE OUR LAWS AND CUSTOMS...

THEY KEPT US IN THE CHURCH ALMOST ALL NIGHT.

FINALLY, AROUND 4:30 IN THE MORNING, WE WERE ALLOWED TO LEAVE.

THE NEXT DAY, A JUDGE **LIFTED** THE INJUNCTION AGAINST THE FREEDOM RIDERS. WE MET THAT EVENING TO ORGANIZE THE CONTINUATION OF THE RIDES.

JAMES FARMER WAS TALKING A LOT, TRYING TO TAKE CONTROL. BUT IT RUBBED A LOT OF PEOPLE THE WRONG WAY.

ANOTHER ISSUE WAS DR. KING'S PARTICIPATION IN THE RIDES.

MARTIN, ARE YOU GOING TO JOIN US? WILL YOU RIDE WITH US?

I CAN'T GO, DIANE.

I'M STILL ON **PROBATION** FROM MY ARREST IN ATLANTA.

I'm on probation, too!

me too!

same here.

yeah

WE'RE ALL ON PROBATION, DR. KING.

MONTGOMERY, AL--
MAY 23, 1961.

THE NEXT DAY WE HELD A
PRESS CONFERENCE ANNOUNCING
OUR INTENTION TO CONTINUE
THE FREEDOM RIDES TO
JACKSON, MISSISSIPPI--
THE HEART OF THE BEAST.

91

JACKSON, MS-- MAY 24, 1961

WHEN WE GOT TO THE JACKSON BUS STATION, WE LEARNED THAT EVERYONE FROM THE BUS AHEAD OF US HAD ALREADY BEEN TAKEN TO JAIL.

WHITE WAITING

COLORED WAITING

BUT THAT DIDN'T STOP US.

WHITES ONLY

WHITE MEN'S RESTROOM

WHEN I ASK YOU A QUESTION, YOU FINISH YOUR ANSWERS WITH "SIR" BECAUSE I AM YOUR SUPERIOR.

DO YOU UNDERSTAND ME?!

INSTEAD, MUCH OF THE MEANS OF ENFORCING SEGREGATION CAME THROUGH ECONOMIC AND POLITICAL PRESSURE ORGANIZED BY A GROUP CALLED THE WHITE CITIZENS' COUNCIL.

BUT BEHIND CLOSED DOORS--

SORT OF LIKE A BUSINESSMAN'S KU KLUX KLAN.

yes.

GOD DAMMIT!

THE VIOLENCE COULD BE EVEN WORSE.

WE WERE QUICKLY TAKEN TO TRIAL. THE PROSECUTION ONLY CALLED ONE WITNESS, AND ALL **27** OF US WERE CONVICTED OF DISTURBING THE PEACE. WE WERE SENTENCED TO A $200 FINE EACH, AND A SUSPENDED SENTENCE OF **60 DAYS** IN JAIL.

REFUSING TO PAY THE FINE MEANT THAT WE WOULD **HAVE** TO SERVE OUR 60 DAYS IN JAIL. FOR MANY, THAT WAS A VERY FRIGHTENING PROSPECT.

BUT FOR ME, AND NEARLY EVERY OTHER FREEDOM RIDER, WE JUST WOULD **NOT** PAY THAT FINE.

AND SO WE WENT TO JAIL.

THREE DAYS AFTER OUR TRIAL, WE WERE TRANSFERRED TO HINDS COUNTY JAIL--

EVEN MORE CROWDED THAN JACKSON CITY HALL'S CELLS.

SOON, WORD MANAGED TO TRICKLE IN ABOUT WHAT WAS HAPPENING ON THE OUTSIDE.

IT ISN'T JUST A RIDE ANYMORE, JOHN--

THEY'RE HAPPENING ALL OVER, FOUR OR FIVE HERE, A DOZEN MORE THERE-- ALL GETTING ON BUSES TO JACKSON.

WE'LL SEE 'EM IN HERE WITH US BEFORE TOO LONG.

WITHIN TWO WEEKS OF OUR ARRIVAL IN HINDS COUNTY, THE GROWING NUMBER OF FREEDOM RIDERS BEING HOUSED WITHIN ITS WALLS FORCED THE LOCAL SHERIFF TO TRANSFER US TO ANOTHER PRISON...

take off your shoes. then take off all your clothing.

IT WAS DEHUMANIZING,

AS WAS OUR BEING FORCED TO SHAVE ALL OF OUR FACIAL HAIR AS PART OF AN EFFORT TO STRIP AWAY OUR DIGNITY--

--OUR VERY HUMANITY.

SHOWERS.

Come on, man. no underwear?

WHAT'S THIS HANG-UP ABOUT CLOTHES?

BUT THE ALWAYS-COLORFUL JIM BEVEL HELPED KEEP IT IN PERSPECTIVE.

GANDHI WRAPPED A RAG AROUND HIS BALLS AND BROUGHT DOWN THE WHOLE BRITISH EMPIRE.

107

IN MISSISSIPPI, THOSE CHARGED WITH BREACH OF THE PEACE, AS WE WERE, HAD TO POST BOND WITHIN 40 DAYS OR LOSE ANY RIGHT TO APPEAL.

THUP

SO, THREE WEEKS AND A DAY AFTER WE'D ARRIVED,

AND WELL MORE THAN A MONTH AFTER WE'D BEEN ARRESTED IN JACKSON,

IT WAS A COMPLETE SURPRISE TO US

WHEN BOND WAS POSTED ON OUR BEHALF

AND WE WERE SET FREE.

EXIT

BY THE END OF THE SUMMER, DOZENS **MORE** BUSES CARRIED THE NATION'S DAUGHTERS AND SONS INTO THE HEART OF THE DEEP SOUTH TO CARRY ON THE WORK WE BEGAN.

THE FARE WAS PAID IN BLOOD, BUT THE FREEDOM RIDES STIRRED THE NATIONAL CONSCIOUSNESS AND AWOKE THE HEARTS AND MINDS OF A GENERATION.

THE FEDERAL GOVERNMENT RESPONDED. ATTORNEY GENERAL ROBERT KENNEDY AND THE JUSTICE DEPARTMENT PETITIONED THE INTERSTATE COMMERCE COMMISSION (ICC) FOR A RULING TO ENFORCE THE SUPREME COURT'S DECISION IN **BOYNTON**, AND IT CAME ON SEPTEMBER 22nd, 1961.

WE WERE BECOMING A NATIONAL MOVEMENT.

AFTER WE WERE RELEASED FROM PARCHMAN, I WENT BACK TO NASHVILLE, WHERE THE NATIONAL ATTENTION HAD CAUSED OUR NUMBERS TO SWELL.

THE SUCCESS OF OUR CAMPAIGN TO DESEGREGATE THE MOVIE THEATERS THERE LED US TO SHIFT OUR EFFORTS FROM INTEGRATION OF FACILITIES TO FAIR EMPLOYMENT PRACTICES, AS PART OF WHAT WE CALLED "OPERATION OPEN CITY."

THIS TIME WE WERE JOINED BY A NUMBER OF PEOPLE FROM OUT OF TOWN, MOSTLY NORTHERNERS COMING OR GOING FROM THE FREEDOM RIDES.

HEY--

SO YOU WANNA BE **BLACK**?

THUGS WERE HIRED TO HARASS US.

WELL, TAKE **THIS**!

PSHHHHHHTTTT

thank you.

I DEEPLY BELIEVE THAT OUR **DISCIPLINE** PAVED THE ROAD TO OUR SUCCESS.

BUT I WAS STARTING TO SEE THAT DISCIPLINE ERODE.

WHAT ARE YOU LOOKING AT?!

I LOST COUNT OF THE NUMBER OF TIMES I HAD TO TAKE SOMEONE ASIDE.

WHAT ARE YOU **DOING**?!

THAT'S WHAT I THOUGHT.

ONE OF THE PEOPLE PASSING THROUGH TOWN WHO ACTED OUT THE MOST WAS STOKELY CARMICHAEL.

THAT IS **NOT** HOW WE PROTEST IN NASHVILLE!

STOKELY LATER SAID HE NEVER SAW IT AS HIS RESPONSIBILITY TO BE THE MORAL AND SPIRITUAL RECLAMATION OF SOME RACIST THUG.

BUT HIS BEHAVIOR WAS THREATENING TO **DERAIL** OUR EFFORTS.

OUR CENTRAL COMMITTEE HELD A MEETING, AND THE RESPONSIBILITY FELL TO JIM LAWSON TO INFORM STOKELY OF THE DECISION.

THE COMMITTEE WOULD LIKE TO OFFER YOU AN INVITATION TO CONTINUE YOUR PROTEST ACTIVITIES...

...ELSEWHERE.

IN JUNE OF 1961, ROBERT KENNEDY SUGGESTED TO DIANE NASH AND OTHERS THAT IT WOULD BE A BETTER DECISION FOR US, IN THE LONG RUN, TO FOCUS ON REGISTERING BLACK VOTERS.

I BELIEVED OUR DIRECT ACTION CAMPAIGNS WERE WORKING, AND MANY WITHIN THE MOVEMENT WERE UPSET AT THE MERE SUGGESTION. BUT BY THE END OF 1961, DR. KING GAVE THE IDEA HIS FULL ENDORSEMENT.

THE CENTRAL FRONT IS THAT OF **SUFFRAGE.** IF WE IN THE SOUTH CAN WIN THE RIGHT TO VOTE, IT WILL PLACE IN OUR HANDS MORE THAN AN ABSTRACT RIGHT--

IT WILL GIVE US THE CONCRETE TOOL WITH WHICH WE, **OURSELVES,** CAN CORRECT INJUSTICE.

THERE WAS A GREAT D I V I D E WITHIN SNCC.

A COMPROMISE SUGGESTED BY ELLA BAKER WAS AGREED TO, CREATING TWO WINGS--

ONE, FOCUSED ON DIRECT ACTION, WAS LED BY DIANE NASH. THE OTHER, FOCUSED ON VOTER REGISTRATION, WAS LED BY CHARLIE JONES.

A BIRD NEEDS TWO WINGS TO **FLY.**

A PLAN QUICKLY TOOK SHAPE FOR SNCC TO SEND FIELD SECRETARIES INTO COMMUNITIES THROUGHOUT THE SOUTH TO ORGANIZE AND REGISTER AMERICA'S BLACK VOTE.

WHEN AMZIE MOORE, A FILLING STATION OWNER AND LOCAL ORGANIZER FROM CLEVELAND, MISSISSIPPI, CAME TO OUR SNCC MEETING AND ASKED US TO SEND HELP,

BOB MOSES, A SOFT-SPOKEN 26-YEAR-OLD FROM HARLEM WITH A GRADUATE DEGREE IN PHILOSOPHY FROM HARVARD, WAS THE HELP THAT ARRIVED.

(CLEVELAND WASN'T FAR FROM MONEY, MISSISSIPPI, WHERE JUST SIX YEARS EARLIER EMMETT TILL'S MUTILATED BODY WAS PULLED FROM THE WATERS OF THE TALLAHATCHIE.)

NO STATE SHOWED US WHAT WE WERE UP AGAINST MORE THAN MISSISSIPPI. NEARLY **90 PERCENT** OF THE STATE'S BLACK FAMILIES LIVED BELOW THE POVERTY LINE, AND ONLY **5 PERCENT** OF ELIGIBLE BLACK VOTERS WERE REGISTERED.

IN MANY COUNTIES, THERE WERE **NONE**.

THE GOOD LORD WAS THE ORIGINAL **SEGREGATIONIST**.

HE PUT THE NEGRO IN AFRICA, SEPARATED HIM FROM ALL OTHER RACES.

(GOVERNOR ROSS BARNETT, 1960-1964)

114

IN LIBERTY, MISSISSIPPI, A LOCAL BLACK FARMER NAMED HERBERT LEE WHO STARTED WORKING WITH BOB MOSES TO HELP REGISTER VOTERS WAS SHOT DEAD BY E.H. HURST--

A MEMBER OF THE MISSISSIPPI STATE LEGISLATURE.

HURST CLAIMED LEE HAD ATTACKED HIM WITH A TIRE IRON, AND SO HURST SHOT HIM THROUGH THE HEAD.

NOT GUILTY BY REASON OF JUSTIFIABLE HOMICIDE.

THE SOLE BLACK WITNESS LATER SAID HE LIED IN TESTIMONY BECAUSE HE WAS SCARED FOR HIS OWN LIFE.

BOB MOSES, CHARLES McDEW, AND A WHITE SNCC MEMBER FROM ALABAMA NAMED BOB ZELLNER LED A PROTEST MARCH IN RESPONSE TO THE VERDICT.

THEY WERE BEATEN BY A MOB BEFORE BEING ARRESTED ALONG WITH 119 LOCAL STUDENTS.

THE PROTESTORS WERE SENTENCED TO FOUR MONTHS IN PRISON.

JUSTICE FOR HERBERT LEE

115

MEANWHILE--

I ENROLLED AT FISK UNIVERSITY AND WAS ELECTED CHAIRMAN OF THE NASHVILLE MOVEMENT, BUT BY THEN DIANE AND BEVEL WERE WORKING DOWN IN JACKSON, AND MOST EVERYONE FROM THOSE EARLY MEETINGS WITH JIM LAWSON HAD MOVED ON.

I FELT A LITTLE LIKE AN OUTSIDER.

A NUMBER OF PROFESSORS, AND EVEN SOME OF MY CLASSMATES, THOUGHT I WAS A LITTLE ODD -- AND I DID TAKE A LIGHT COURSE LOAD TO FOCUS ON MY PRIORITY, THE MOVEMENT.

BUT I WILL NEVER FORGET GATHERING ONE AFTERNOON THAT NOVEMBER TO GO DOWNTOWN FOR A DEMONSTRATION.

HOWMM

ARF!

woof! woof!

ARF!

WE WERE GETTING SET TO DRIVE OVER TO FIRST BAPTIST WHEN WE HEARD A COMMOTION.

woof woof! whimper whimper RUFF!

I WAS SHOCKED TO SEE THESE YOUNG BLACK FRATERNITY MEN SWEPT UP LIKE THIS, AT THE VERY MOMENT THAT PEOPLE THEIR OWN AGE WERE RISKING THEIR LIVES.

IN APRIL 1962, **SNCC** HELD A CONFERENCE IN ATLANTA TO OBSERVE ITS SECOND ANNIVERSARY.

come S.N.C.C. Conference
APRIL-27-29
ATLANTA STUDENT MOVEMENT~

IT WAS INCREDIBLE TO SEE HOW DRASTICALLY THE ORGANIZATION HAD CHANGED IN SUCH A SHORT TIME.

BERNARD, BEVEL, DIANE, AND OTHERS WERE NOW GONE. IN THEIR PLACE ROSE NEW VOICES--

STOKELY CARMICHAEL, JIM FORMAN, CHARLES SHERROD, RUBY SMITH, AND WHITE ACTIVISTS FROM LEFTIST GROUPS SUCH AS THE SOUTHERN CONFERENCE EDUCATIONAL FUND AND STUDENTS FOR A DEMOCRATIC SOCIETY (SDS).

OUR CAUSE REMAINED THE SAME, BUT OUR METHODS WERE IN QUESTION.

WE FORGET TOO SOON THE JAILINGS AND BEATINGS SUFFERED BY OUR BROTHERS AND SISTERS FIGHTING EVERY DAY.

MORE THAN A FEW OF THE 250 SNCC REPRESENTATIVES IN ATLANTA THAT WEEKEND ARGUED THAT IT SHOULD BE ACCEPTABLE TO STRIKE BACK IF YOU'RE HIT.

APRIL-27-29
ANTA STUDENT MOVEMEN

IF WE ARE MET WITH VIOLENCE, WE MUST BE ABLE TO DEFEND OURSELVES.

117

JIM LAWSON WOULD **NEVER** ACCEPT SUCH A POSITION, BUT HE WASN'T THERE TO OFFER HIS OWN. FOR THE FIRST TIME, LAWSON, WHO HAD BEEN SO CRUCIAL TO THE CREATION OF **SNCC** -- THE VERY **AUTHOR** OF THE STATEMENT OF PURPOSE PRINTED ON THE CONFERENCE'S BROCHURE--

--WAS NOT INVITED TO PARTICIPATE.

STUDENT NONVIOLENT COORDINATING COMMITTEE

STATEMENT OF PURPOSE

We affirm the philosophical or religious ideal of nonviolence as the foundation of our purpose, the presupposition of our faith, and the manner of our action. Nonviolence as it grows from Judaic-Christian traditions seeks a social order of justice permeated by love. Integration of human endeavor represents the crucial first step towards such a society.

Through nonviolence, courage displaces fear; love transforms hate. Acceptance dissipates prejudice; hope ends despair. Peace dominates war; faith reconciles doubt. Mutual regard cancels enmity. Justice for all overthrows injustice. The redemptive community supersedes systems of gross social immorality.

Love is the central motif of nonviolence. Love is the force by which God binds man to Himself and man to man. Such love goes to the extreme; it remains loving and forgiving even in the midst of hostility. It matches the capacity of evil to inflict suffering with an even more enduring capacity to absorb evil, all the while persisting in love.

By appealing to conscience and standing on the moral nature of human existence, nonviolence nurtures the atmosphere in which reconciliation and justice become actual possibilities.

EVERYONE KNEW I STOOD WITH JIM WHEN IT CAME TO NONVIOLENCE,

BUT THE FACT THAT I'D BEEN ARRESTED AND BEATEN AND JAILED SO MANY TIMES HELD A LOT OF WEIGHT WITH MY **SNCC** COLLEAGUES, OLD AND NEW.

SO AT THE SAME TIME AS JIM LAWSON WAS **SHUNNED**, I WAS ELECTED TO SNCC'S EXECUTIVE COORDINATING COMMITTEE.

CAIRO, ILLINOIS.

NEAR THE END OF THE SUMMER OF 1962, I WAS LEADING A PROTEST AT THE CAIRO SWIMMING POOL, WHICH HAD REMAINED **SEGREGATED** DESPITE OUR WEEKS OF DEMONSTRATION.

DANNY LYON, A NEW STAFF PHOTOGRAPHER FOR SNCC -- WE CALLED HIM **DANDELION** -- WAS THERE THAT DAY.

CLICK CLICK

AS WE KNELT AND PRAYED, DANNY SNAPPED A PHOTOGRAPH.

THAT PICTURE BECAME PROBABLY THE MOST POPULAR POSTER OF THE MOVEMENT.

WHAT A LOT OF PEOPLE **DON'T** KNOW IS WHAT HAPPENED JUST AFTER THAT PHOTO WAS TAKEN.

RRR

outta the way!!

he isn't stopping!

THAT SEPTEMBER, THE NATION WATCHED AS MORE THAN **300** U.S. MARSHALS WERE WOUNDED TRYING TO PROTECT **JAMES MEREDITH** AS HE BECAME THE FIRST AFRICAN-AMERICAN TO ENROLL AT THE UNIVERSITY OF MISSISSIPPI.

IN NOVEMBER, I ATTENDED A **SNCC** CONFERENCE IN NASHVILLE.

THOSE MOBS DOWN IN MISSISSIPPI MAKE YOUR PROTESTS **HERE** LOOK LIKE SMALL POTATOES, JOHN.

HE WASN'T WRONG.

AS PART OF THE CONFERENCE, WE STAGED A DEMONSTRATION AT THE **TIC-TOC**, A SEGREGATED RESTAURANT.

BUT THIS PROTEST LACKED DISCIPLINE--

SOMETHING I WAS SEEING MORE AND MORE OFTEN.

YOUNG MAN, WE DON'T ALLOW SMOKING HERE.

square.

STUBBS

AND IT WASN'T THE ONLY PROBLEM FESTERING WITHIN SNCC.

BY THE END OF 1962, YOU HEARD PEOPLE QUESTIONING WHETHER SNCC SHOULD EVEN BE A MULTI-RACIAL ORGANIZATION.

JANUARY 14, 1963.
ALABAMA STATE CAPITOL.

KLOP
KLOP
KLOP

INAUGURATION OF **GEORGE CORLEY WALLACE, JR.,** 45th GOVERNOR OF ALABAMA

TODAY I HAVE STOOD WHERE ONCE JEFFERSON DAVIS STOOD, AND TOOK AN OATH TO MY PEOPLE.

EVEN AS WALLACE WAS SPEAKING THAT DAY, DR. KING'S ORGANIZATION THE **SOUTHERN CHRISTIAN LEADERSHIP CONFERENCE (SCL** HELD A MEETING TO DECIDE WHAT TO DO.

IT IS VERY APPROPRIATE THEN, THAT FROM THIS CRADLE OF THE CONFEDERACY, THE VERY **HEART** OF THE GREAT ANGLO-SAXON SOUTHLAND, THAT TODAY WE SOUND THE DRUM FOR FREEDOM, AS HAVE OUR GENERATIONS OF FOREBEARS BEFORE US HAVE DONE, TIME AND TIME AGAIN THROUGHOUT **HISTORY.**

LET US RISE TO THE CALL OF FREEDOM-LOVING BLOOD THAT IS IN US, AND SEND OUR ANSWER TO THE **TYRANNY** THAT CLANKS ITS CHAINS UPON THE SOUTH.

IN THE NAME OF THE GREATEST PEOPLE THAT HAVE EVER TROD THIS EARTH, I DRAW THE LINE IN THE DUST,

THEY NEEDED A NEW **TARGET**--

THEY "NEEDED A VICTORY", AS FRED SHUTTLESWORTH PUT IT.

AND TOSS THE GAUNTLET BEFORE THE FEET OF **TYRANNY.**

AND I SAY--

AND SO **THE BIRMINGHAM CAMPAIGN** BEGAN THE FIRST WEEK OF APRIL.

DR. KING AND **SCLC** BROUGHT IN PEOPLE FROM ALL CORNERS OF THE MOVEMENT. DIANE AND BEVEL WENT TO HELP ORGANIZE VOLUNTEERS AND **TRAIN** THEM IN OUR TECHNIQUES.

EVEN **AL HIBBLER,** A FAMOUS JAZZ SINGER WHO HAPPENED TO BE BLIND, JOINED THE PROTESTS.

WE COULD _NEVER_ JUST LEAVE A BLIND MAN ALONE ON A STREET CORNER...

THE NEXT DAY.

NOT MUCH HAD CHANGED IN THE TWO YEARS SINCE THE FREEDOM RIDE CAME THROUGH BIRMINGHAM...

127

AFTER WEEKS OF NIGHTLY MASS MEETINGS TO COORDINATE THE PROTESTS, DR. KING ANNOUNCED THAT HE WOULD PERSONALLY LEAD THE NEXT MARCH.

8:30 P.M.-- ST. JAMES AME CHURCH.

WE ARE NOT HERE TO DO SOMETHING FOR YOU, BUT TO DO SOMETHING **WITH** YOU. WE WILL MARCH THROUGH THE STREETS OF BIRMINGHAM WITH YOU. **EVERYONE** IN THE MOVEMENT MUST LIVE A SACRIFICIAL LIFE.

...FOR A MOVE FOR FREEDOM.

I CAN'T THINK OF A BETTER DAY THAN **GOOD FRIDAY**...

FRIDAY, APRIL 12, 1963. ZION HILL BAPTIST CHURCH-- BIRMINGHAM, AL.

all right folks, we're moving out! remember

THERE HE GOES, JUST LIKE JESUS.

Yes!

CONNOR HAD OBTAINED A COURT ORDER FROM THE STATE PROHIBITING **ALL** PROTEST ACTIVITIES, AND SET THE BOND AT **EIGHT TIMES** THE NORMAL MAXIMUM.

EVERYONE KNEW THAT THIS MARCH WOULD MEAN **JAIL TIME**.

SOME WERE CONCERNED THAT THE CAMPAIGN WOULD **COLLAPSE** IF DR. KING WENT TO PRISON.

STOP THEM THERE.

HALT!

ERRRT

SCREEE

CLIK CLIK CLIK

PFASH!

WHEN DR. KING WAS ARRESTED ON GOOD FRIDAY, HE WAS CRITICIZED BY SOME OF THE AREA'S LIBERAL AND MODERATE WHITE LEADERSHIP FOR STOKING CONFLICT BY LEADING THESE DEMONSTRATIONS.

HIS RESPONSE, WRITTEN ON SCRAPS OF PAPER AND SMUGGLED OUT OF HIS CELL, WAS THE "LETTER FROM BIRMINGHAM JAIL."

"...I SUBMIT THAT AN INDIVIDUAL WHO BREAKS A LAW THAT CONSCIENCE TELLS HIM IS **UNJUST**, AND WHO WILLINGLY ACCEPTS THE PENALTY OF IMPRISONMENT IN ORDER TO AROUSE THE CONSCIENCE OF THE **COMMUNITY** OVER ITS INJUSTICE, IS IN REALITY EXPRESSING THE HIGHEST **RESPECT** FOR LAW."

IT WAS AN **EMBARRASSMENT** TO THE CITY.

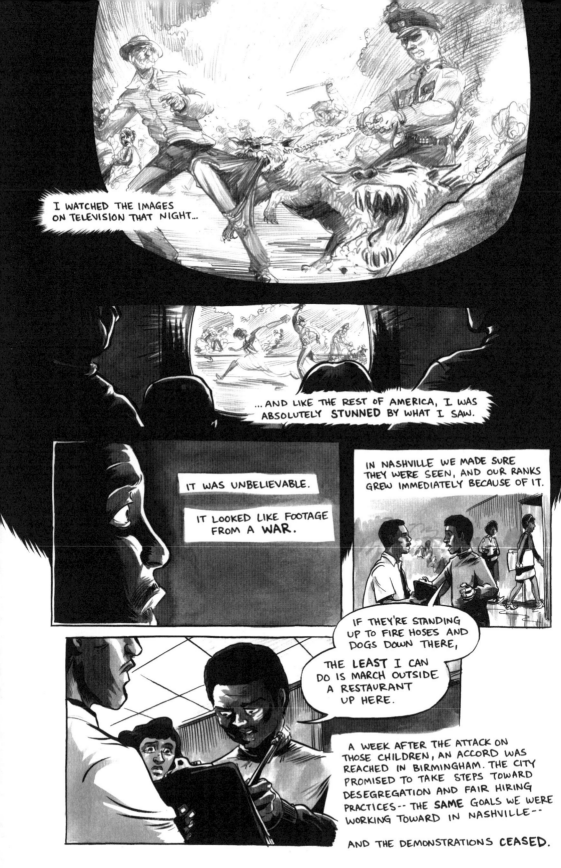

I WATCHED THE IMAGES ON TELEVISION THAT NIGHT...

...AND LIKE THE REST OF AMERICA, I WAS ABSOLUTELY STUNNED BY WHAT I SAW.

IT WAS UNBELIEVABLE.

IT LOOKED LIKE FOOTAGE FROM A WAR.

IN NASHVILLE WE MADE SURE THEY WERE SEEN, AND OUR RANKS GREW IMMEDIATELY BECAUSE OF IT.

IF THEY'RE STANDING UP TO FIRE HOSES AND DOGS DOWN THERE,

THE LEAST I CAN DO IS MARCH OUTSIDE A RESTAURANT UP HERE.

A WEEK AFTER THE ATTACK ON THOSE CHILDREN, AN ACCORD WAS REACHED IN BIRMINGHAM. THE CITY PROMISED TO TAKE STEPS TOWARD DESEGREGATION AND FAIR HIRING PRACTICES-- THE SAME GOALS WE WERE WORKING TOWARD IN NASHVILLE--

AND THE DEMONSTRATIONS CEASED.

HE WAS COMING HOME FROM A MEETING,

WALKING UP HIS DRIVEWAY,

AND THEY **SHOT** HIM.

who... who shot him?

:sniff: no one knows.

they said it was a SNIPER.

THEY CAN GET **ANYONE**. YOU'LL NEVER SEE IT COMING.

ONE DAY YOU PARK YOUR CAR IN THE DRIVEWAY AND YOU GO INSIDE, AND YOU'RE **FINE**. THE NEXT DAY, YOU COME HOME AND... YOU NEVER MAKE IT TO YOUR DOOR.

JUST LIKE THAT.

LAST NIGHT, PRESIDENT KENNEDY ADDRESSED THE NATION IN RESPONSE TO RECENT EVENTS IN BIRMINGHAM, ALABAMA AND ELSEWHERE:

--THE EVENTS IN BIRMINGHAM AND ELSEWHERE HAVE SO INCREASED THE CRIES FOR EQUALITY THAT NO CITY OR STATE LEGISLATIVE BODY CAN PRUDENTLY IGNORE THEM.

THE FIRES OF FRUSTRATION AND DISCORD ARE BURNING IN EVERY CITY, NORTH **AND** SOUTH.

WE FACE, THEREFORE, A **MORAL CRISIS** AS A COUNTRY AND AS A PEOPLE. IT **CANNOT** BE MET BY REPRESSIVE POLICE ACTION. IT CANNOT BE LEFT TO INCREASED DEMONSTRATIONS ON THE STREETS. IT CANNOT BE **QUIETED** BY TOKEN MOVES OR TALKS.

IT IS TIME TO **ACT** IN CONGRESS, IN YOUR STATE AND LOCAL LEGISLATIVE BODIES-- IN ALL OF OUR **DAILY LIVES**...

A GREAT CHANGE IS AT HAND, AND OUR TASK-- OUR **OBLIGATION**-- IS TO MAKE THAT REVOLUTION, THAT CHANGE, PEACEFUL AND CONSTRUCTIVE FOR ALL.

ALMOST LOST THAT WEEK WAS DR. KING'S ANNOUNCEMENT ON JUNE 11th OF PLANS FOR A **MASSIVE MARCH** TO TAKE PLACE LATER THAT SUMMER...

... IN **WASHINGTON, D.C.**

JUNE 14, 1963-- outside MURFREESBORO, TN.

TWO DAYS LATER, I RECEIVED A TELEGRAM FROM SNCC HEADQUARTERS, SAYING CHUCK McDEW WAS **RESIGNING** AS CHAIRMAN,

AND THAT I SHOULD HURRY TO ATLANTA FOR AN "EMERGENCY" MEETING OF THE COORDINATING COMMITTEE.

IT SEEMED STRANGE TO ME--

141

SKREEE!

I SAW MYSELF AS A **DOER**. I NEVER HAD ANY THOUGHTS OF BEING CHAIRMAN.

THERE WERE NO SEATBELTS IN THAT CAR, BUT INCREDIBLY NONE OF US WERE SERIOUSLY HURT.

RZZZZZ

WE MADE IT, EVENTUALLY.
ANOTHER CAR WAS SENT TO PICK US UP.

AND I WAS ELECTED **CHAIRMAN OF SNCC.**

I WAS BARELY THERE A WEEK WHEN A REPRESENTATIVE OF SNCC WAS INVITED TO THE **WHITE HOUSE** TO JOIN OTHER LEADERS, DISCUSSING PRESIDENT KENNEDY'S PROPOSED CIVIL **RIGHTS BILL** AS WELL AS HIS CONCERNS ABOUT THE ANNOUNCEMENT OF A **MARCH ON WASHINGTON.**

AMONG THE SNCC MEMBERS, THERE WASN'T MUCH INTEREST IN THE MARCH **OR** PRESIDENT KENNEDY'S BILL.

MANY THOUGHT THE MARCH WOULD BE A LAME EVENT STAGED BY CONSERVATIVE BLACK LEADERS THAT WAS PROBABLY, IN SOME WAY, CONTROLLED BY THE FEDERAL GOVERNMENT.

AS FOR THE CIVIL RIGHTS BILL-- WE COULD **NOT** SUPPORT IT.

THE KENNEDY BILL DID **NOT** GUARANTEE THE RIGHT OF **ALL** AFRICAN-AMERICANS TO VOTE. THE ADMINISTRATION TOOK THE POSITION THAT, IF YOU HAD A 6th-GRADE EDUCATION, YOU SHOULD BE CONSIDERED **LITERATE** AND ABLE TO VOTE.

SNCC'S POSITION-- AND MINE-- WAS THAT THE **ONLY** QUALIFICATION FOR BEING ABLE TO VOTE SHOULD BE THAT OF **AGE** AND **RESIDENCE.**

HERE, JOHN. YOU'RE THE CHAIRMAN-- YOU **HAVE** TO GO.

SO I WENT.

THE IDEA FOR THE MARCH ON WASHINGTON
CAME FROM A. PHILIP RANDOLPH.

HE WAS A STATESMAN, A TRUE GENTLEMAN.
IN 1925 HE FOUNDED THE **BROTHERHOOD OF
SLEEPING CAR PORTERS,** AN INCREDIBLY
INFLUENTIAL CIVIL RIGHTS AND LABOR
ORGANIZATION. IF HE HAD BEEN BORN AT
ANOTHER TIME, HE COULD'VE BEEN
PRESIDENT. AND I'LL NEVER FORGET
THAT DEEP BARITONE VOICE.

MR. RANDOLPH FIRST THREATENED TO
ORGANIZE A MARCH ON THE CAPITAL
CITY IN 1941 AS HE FACED OFF WITH
PRESIDENT ROOSEVELT OVER WHETHER
OR NOT AFRICAN-AMERICAN WORKERS
WOULD BE INTEGRATED INTO THE
GROWING WAR ECONOMY.

AS A RESULT, PRESIDENT ROOSEVELT
SIGNED AN EXECUTIVE ORDER FORBIDDING
THE DEFENSE INDUSTRY FROM
DISCRIMINATION IN HIRING, AND PLANS
FOR THE MARCH WERE CANCELED.

JUNE 22, 1963-- THE WHITE HOUSE.

THE BLACK MASSES ARE **RESTLESS**, MR. PRESIDENT.

WE ARE **GOING** TO MARCH ON WASHINGTON.

WE WANT SUCCESS IN CONGRESS, NOT JUST A **BIG SHOW** AT THE CAPITOL.

THE NEGROES ARE **ALREADY** IN THE STREETS.

THE CIVIL RIGHTS BILL STANDS A... MUCH BETTER CHANCE IF THE NEGROES STAY **OFF** THE STREETS.

THERE **WILL** BE A MARCH.

MR. RANDOLPH--

IF YOU BRING ALL THESE PEOPLE TO WASHINGTON, WON'T THERE BE VIOLENCE AND CHAOS AND DISORDER?

THERE HAVE BEEN ORDERLY, PEACEFUL, NONVIOLENT PROTESTS BEFORE.

IT WAS **UNREAL**-- I HAD ONLY BEEN CHAIRMAN OF SNCC FOR A **WEEK**, AND HERE I WAS.

THE MEETING WENT ON FOR NEARLY TWO HOURS BEFORE **DR. KING** SPOKE UP FOR THE FIRST TIME.

MR. PRESIDENT--

THERE WAS ONE PERSON DELIBERATELY **NOT** INVITED THAT DAY.
MALCOLM X OF THE NATION OF ISLAM.

I **KNEW** MALCOLM. I **RESPECTED** HIM.

I **SHARED** HIS BELIEF THAT OUR STRUGGLE
WAS NOT SIMPLY IN THE COURTS, BUT
IN THE **STREETS.**

STILL, I NEVER FELT LIKE HE WAS A PART
OF THE MOVEMENT.

OUR MOVEMENT WAS ABOUT CREATING
AN OPEN, INTEGRATED SOCIETY.

AND, VIOLENCE, NO MATTER HOW JUSTIFIED,
WAS **NOT** SOMETHING I COULD ACCEPT.

BUT I COULD UNDERSTAND HIS APPEAL,
AND THE FEELINGS OF RESTLESSNESS
THAT DROVE IT.

JULY 2, 1963.

A MEETING OF THE MARCH ORGANIZERS WAS CALLED IN NEW YORK CITY. IT WAS THE FIRST TIME I HAD EVER BEEN THERE.

I'M SORRY, BUT YOU HAVE TO LEAVE. thank you.

BUT I

uh huh, yes, YOU TOO -- YOU CAN WAIT OUTSIDE. oh--

JOHN, YOU CAN **STAY**.

?!

I WAS SHOCKED AT THE WAY ROY WILKINS WAS ABLE TO PUSH EVERYONE AROUND.

come on in, everyone's here.

ONLY THE SIX OF US WHO MET WITH THE PRESIDENT REMAINED.

I DIDN'T KNOW IT AT THE TIME, BUT THOSE OF US IN THAT ROOM--

A. PHILIP RANDOLPH,

DR. MARTIN LUTHER KING, JR.,

ROY WILKINS of the NAACP,

JIM FARMER of CORE,

and WHITNEY YOUNG of the URBAN LEAGUE

-- WOULD BE FOREVER LINKED, KNOWN COLLECTIVELY AS THE "BIG SIX".

THANK YOU, ROY.

of course, Mr. Randolph.

scoot.

now--

THE DISCUSSION QUICKLY TURNED TO WHO SHOULD BE LEADING OUR EFFORTS.

AS MANY OF YOU KNOW, I BELIEVE DEEPLY IN THE NECESSITY OF A MARCH ON WASHINGTON, AND I HAVE FOR QUITE SOME TIME.

THERE IS NO ONE, IN MY ESTIMATION, MORE QUALIFIED TO ORGANIZE THIS ENDEAVOR THAN BAYARD RUSTIN.

BAYARD RUSTIN.

HE WAS ONE OF THE PEOPLE ROY WILKINS HAD ASKED TO **LEAVE**, BUT HIS TALENTS LOOMED.

A DEVOUT PACIFIST AND BRILLIANT ORGANIZER, RUSTIN HELPED WITH THE PLANNING OF RANDOLPH'S FIRST MARCH IN 1941.

BUT WILKINS AND WHITNEY YOUNG WERE **OPPOSED**.

I'M TELLING YOU, PEOPLE ARE GOING TO USE HIM **AGAINST** US.

HE'S A CONSCIENTIOUS OBJECTOR, HE'S BEEN LINKED TO THE COMMUNIST PARTY,

and, of course, there's the "MORALS" charge...

RUSTIN WAS GAY, THOUGH NO ONE SAID IT DIRECTLY. IT MADE HIM A STRATEGIC LIABILITY.

WE WERE AT AN IMPASSE UNTIL SOMEONE SUGGESTED A. PHILIP RANDOLPH LEAD THE MARCH.

YES PHIL, YOU **SHOULD** LEAD IT.

IF I DO THAT, I **WILL** CHOOSE BAYARD AS MY DEPUTY.

Well, YOU CAN DO THAT IF YOU **WANT** TO, BUT DON'T EXPECT ME TO DO ANYTHING ABOUT IT WHEN THE **TROUBLE** STARTS.

WE **NEEDED** RUSTIN. HE WAS THE ONLY PERSON WITH THE ABILITY AND CAPACITY TO ORGANIZE SUCH A **MASSIVE** MARCH.

AFTER THE MEETING, WE POSED FOR PICTURES WITH THE PRESS.

DR. KING, WHERE ARE ALL THE YOUNG PEOPLE WE KEEP HEARING ABOUT?

RIGHT THERE-- **JOHN LEWIS**, CHAIRMAN OF SNCC.

YOU SAY THIS MARCH WILL NOT INCLUDE ANY CIVIL DISOBEDIENCE OR SIT-INS. IS SNCC **BACKING AWAY** FROM ITS PROVOCATIVE TACTICS?

NO, WE WILL **NOT** CHANGE OUR TACTICS.

WE DO **NOT** WANT VIOLENCE, AND WE DO NOT ADVOCATE FOR IT--

151

-- BUT WE WILL **NOT** SLOW DOWN BECAUSE OF THE **POSSIBILITY**.

A FEW WEEKS LATER, I WAS INVITED TO CONTRIBUTE TO NEGOTIATIONS FOR A **SNCC-** AFFILIATED PROTEST MOVEMENT IN MARYLAND.

JULY 22, 1963 -- THE JUSTICE DEPARTMENT, WASHINGTON, D.C.

DURING A BREAK, ATTORNEY GENERAL ROBERT KENNEDY PULLED ME ASIDE AND SAID SOMETHING I'LL NEVER FORGET.

A **JARRING** RIGHT HAND--

--THE **KNOCKOUT BLOW!!**

FOLLOWED BY THE LEFT UPPERCUT--

JOHN--

UP TILL THEN, MANY IN THE MOVEMENT--INCLUDING MYSELF-- HAD BEEN CRITICAL OF HIS RESPONSE TO OUR PLEAS FOR FEDERAL INTERVENTION.

YOU, THE YOUNG PEOPLE OF SNCC, HAVE EDUCATED ME.

you have CHANGED me.

now I understand.

IT SHOWED ME SOMETHING ABOUT ROBERT KENNEDY THAT I CAME TO RESPECT: EVEN THOUGH HE COULD BE A LITTLE ROUGH-- RUTHLESS, SOME WOULD SAY--

HE WAS WILLING TO LEARN,

TO GROW,

AND TO **CHANGE**.

THE ATTACKS AND CRITICISM OF THE MARCH WERE FIERCE.

ON AUGUST 13th, WITH HELP FROM **FBI** WIRETAPS, **STROM THURMOND** OF SOUTH CAROLINA SPOKE ON THE SENATE FLOOR, ATTACKING BAYARD RUSTIN FOR BEING GAY AND ENTERING HIS ARREST RECORD INTO THE CONGRESSIONAL RECORD--

-- EFFECTIVELY **OUTING** HIM TO THE ENTIRE NATION.

BUT OUR MOVEMENT WAS TAKING HOLD.

IN THE MONTHS FOLLOWING THE ANNOUNCEMENT OF PRESIDENT KENNEDY'S CIVIL RIGHTS BILL, THERE WERE MORE THAN **800** DEMONSTRATIONS IN 200 CITIES, TWENTY **THOUSAND** ARRESTS,

AND TEN **DEATHS.**

NATIONAL HEADQUARTERS
MARCH ON WASHINGTON
for JOBS & FREEDOM
WED. AUG. 28th

MY RESPONSIBILITIES AS CHAIRMAN OF SNCC TOOK ME ALL OVER THE SOUTH -- GREENWOOD, MISSISSIPPI; PINE BLUFF, ARKANSAS; SOMERVILLE, TENNESSEE; DANVILLE, VIRGINIA; SELMA, ALABAMA -- and ELSEWHERE.

THE WEEKEND BEFORE THE MARCH, I WENT TO THE MARCH'S HEADQUARTERS IN HARLEM.

BAYARD SHOWED **NO** SIGN THE ATTACKS WERE GETTING TO HIM.

WHAT ABOUT THE **LATRINES?!** WE NEED MORE--

WE CAN'T HAVE **ANY** DISORGANIZED PISSING IN THE STREETS OF WASHINGTON!

that's EXACTLY what I asked you for.

-- that's right. AND I DON'T CARE--

FOR HIM, AND FOR **ALL** OF US, IT WAS A RACE AGAINST TIME.

I STARTED WORKING ON MY SPEECH FOR THE MARCH
IN ATLANTA, AT FIRST WITH SNCC STAFFER **NANCY STERN**,
THEN WITH SNCC'S COMMUNICATIONS DIRECTOR
JULIAN BOND, OUR EXECUTIVE SECRETARY **JIM FORMAN**,
AS WELL AS **PRATHIA HALL** AND OTHERS HELPING ME
WORK THROUGH THE EARLY DRAFTS.

BY THE TIME I GOT TO NEW YORK CITY, I WAS WORKING THROUGH THE FINAL DRAFT.
THAT WEEKEND, I SAW A PHOTOGRAPH IN THE NEWSPAPER --

IT STUCK WITH ME.

PROTESTS IN RHODESIA

ONE MAN, ONE VOTE

THERE I WORKED WITH SNCC MEMBERS
COURTLAND COX AND **JOYCE LADNER**,
ONE OF BAYARD'S ASSISTANTS **ELEANOR
HOLMES**, AND OTHERS, TO FINISH
THE SPEECH.

WHEN I ARRIVED IN WASHINGTON, THE CITY WAS **VERY** TENSE.

EVERY POLICE OFFICER IN THE CITY WAS ON DUTY, ARMY PARATROOPERS HAD BEEN PUT ON ALERT, AND THE WASHINGTON SENATORS HAD CANCELED TWO HOME GAMES ON ACCOUNT OF THE MARCH.

I WAS SURPRISED TO SEE **MALCOLM X** IN MY HOTEL LOBBY.

and WHY DID YOU COME?

DING!

WHATEVER BLACK FOLKS DO, MAYBE I DON'T SUPPORT IT, BUT I'M GOING TO **BE** THERE, BROTHER--

'CAUSE THAT'S WHERE I BELONG.

KLIK

I FELT IT WAS A STRONG SPEECH, AND THAT IT REPRESENTED THE POSITION OF **SNCC**.

NOK

KLIK!

good to see you, John.

hello, Bayard.

YOU--

HOW CAN **ANYONE** SAY, "IN GOOD CONSCIENCE WE CANNOT SUBMIT THE ADMINISTRATION'S CIVIL RIGHTS BILL, FOR IT IS TOO LITTLE, TOO LATE.

"YOU TELL US TO **WAIT**, YOU TELL US TO BE **PATIENT**, BUT FOR MANY OF US, PATIENCE IS A **DIRTY** AND **NASTY WORD**"?!

THIS IS OFFENSIVE TO THE CATHOLIC CHURCH.

CATHOLICS **BELIEVE** IN THE WORD "PATIENCE."

WHY?

FINE, WE CAN TAKE IT OUT.

PAYYY...TIENCE.

UNbelievable!

good.

IT'S LATE-- THIS IS ENOUGH FOR NOW.

I'M SURE THERE WILL BE MORE, ONCE THE OTHERS HAVE SEEN YOUR SPEECH.

I WILL LISTEN, BUT I CAN'T MAKE ANY PROMISES.

GET SOME REST--

WE HAVE A BIG DAY AHEAD OF US TOMORROW.

157

AUGUST 28, 1963.

THE NEXT MORNING, WE HAD BREAKFAST TOGETHER BEFORE HEADING AS A GROUP TO MEET WITH MEMBERS OF CONGRESSIONAL LEADERSHIP.

NO ONE MENTIONED MY SPEECH.

THE MEETINGS WERE QUICK.

NOTHING SUBSTANTIVE WAS DISCUSSED.

THEN WE LEARNED THAT THE MARCH HAD STARTED **WITHOUT** US.

WE CLEARED A SPACE TO TAKE PICTURES, BUT WE WERE **NOT** AT THE FRONT OF THE MARCH.

TRUTH BE TOLD, WE COULDN'T EVEN **SEE** THE FRONT.

AS THE CROWDS GATHERED, THE PROGRAM BEGAN WITH MUSIC FROM SOME TRULY UNBELIEVABLE PERFORMERS--

YOU JUST **CAN'T SAY** "REVOLUTION" OR "MASSES".

IT'S COMMUNIST TALK.

THERE'S NOTHING **WRONG** WITH THOSE TWO WORDS-- I'VE USED THEM MANY TIMES MYSELF.

AFTER THAT, WE HAD TO **STOP**-- RANDOLPH NEEDED TO GIVE HIS SPEECH OPENING THE OFFICIAL PROGRAM.

BY THE TIME HE RETURNED, THE LIST OF OBJECTIONS HAD GROWN. COURTLAND COX AND JIM FORMAN HAD HEARD WHAT WAS HAPPENING, AND CAME TO THE TENT TO JOIN ME.

WHAT **IS** ALL THIS?!!

IF THERE'S GONNA BE **ONE** MORE WORD CHANGED, IT'S GONNA BE OVER **MY DEAD BODY**!

hey now, charles!

I HAVE WAITED TWENTY-TWO YEARS FOR THIS.

I'VE WAITED ALL MY **LIFE** FOR THIS OPPORTUNITY.

please don't ruin it.

FINALLY, AS THE TIME FOR MY SPEECH CAME NEAR...

JOHN, WE'VE COME THIS FAR TOGETHER.

LET US **STAY** TOGETHER.

OKAY, SIR, WE'LL MAKE THE CHANGES.

I SIMPLY COULD **NOT** SAY NO TO MR. RANDOLPH.

IN THE END, MY SPEECH NO LONGER CALLED THE PRESIDENT'S BILL "TOO LITTLE, TOO LATE", NOR CALLED FOR A "MARCH THROUGH THE HEART OF DIXIE, THE WAY SHERMAN DID."

IT NO LONGER ASKED, "WHICH SIDE IS THE GOVERNMENT ON?", NOR DESCRIBED SOME POLITICAL LEADERS AS "CHEAP."

BUT WHEN WE WERE FINISHED, I WAS STILL SATISFIED WITH THE SPEECH, AS WERE FORMAN AND COX.

WE ALL AGREED THAT OUR MESSAGE WAS **NOT** COMPROMISED.

WE **MUST** HAVE LEGISLATION THAT WILL PROTECT THE MISSISSIPPI SHARECROPPER WHO IS PUT OFF HIS FARM BECAUSE HE **DARES** TO REGISTER TO VOTE.

MY FRIENDS, LET US NOT FORGET THAT WE ARE INVOLVED IN A SERIOUS **SOCIAL REVOLUTION**--

WE **NEED** A BILL THAT WILL PROVIDE FOR THE HOMELESS AND **STARVING** PEOPLE OF THIS NATION.

BY AND LARGE, AMERICAN POLITICS IS DOMINATED BY POLITICIANS WHO BUILD THEIR CAREERS ON **IMMORAL** COMPROMISES, AND ALLY THEMSELVES WITH OPEN FORMS OF POLITICAL, ECONOMIC, AND SOCIAL **EXPLOITATION**.

WE **NEED** A BILL THAT WILL ENSURE THE EQUALITY OF A MAID WHO EARNS **FIVE DOLLARS A WEEK** IN A HOME OF A FAMILY WHOSE TOTAL INCOME IS $100,000 A YEAR. WE MUST HAVE A GOOD **FEPC** BILL.

THERE ARE EXCEPTIONS, OF COURSE. WE **SALUTE** THOSE.

BUT WHAT POLITICAL LEADER CAN STAND UP AND SAY, "MY PARTY IS THE PARTY OF PRINCIPLES"?

FOR THE PARTY OF **KENNEDY** IS ALSO THE PARTY OF EASTLAND. THE PARTY OF JAVITS IS ALSO THE PARTY OF **GOLDWATER**.

WHERE IS **OUR** PARTY?!

WHERE IS THE POLITICAL PARTY THAT WILL MAKE IT <u>UNNECESSARY</u> TO MARCH ON WASHINGTON?!

WHERE IS THE POLITICAL PARTY THAT WILL MAKE IT UNNECESSARY TO MARCH IN THE STREETS OF BIRMINGHAM?

WHERE IS THE POLITICAL PARTY THAT WILL PROTECT THE CITIZENS OF ALBANY, GEORGIA?

DO YOU KNOW THAT IN ALBANY, GEORGIA, **NINE** OF OUR LEADERS HAVE BEEN INDICTED **NOT** BY THE **DIXIECRATS**, BUT BY THE **FEDERAL GOVERNMENT**, FOR PEACEFUL PROTEST?

BUT WHAT DID THE FEDERAL GOVERNMENT DO WHEN ALBANY'S DEPUTY SHERIFF **BEAT** ATTORNEY **C.B. KING** AND LEFT HIM HALF-DEAD?

WHAT DID THE FEDERAL GOVERNMENT DO WHEN LOCAL POLICE OFFICIALS KICKED AND ASSAULTED THE **PREGNANT** WIFE OF SLATER KING,

and she lost her baby?

TO THOSE WHO HAVE SAID, "**BE PATIENT AND WAIT**," WE HAVE LONG SAID THAT WE **CANNOT** BE PATIENT.

WE DO **NOT** WANT OUR FREEDOM GRADUALLY, BUT WE WANT TO BE FREE **NOW**!

WE ARE **TIRED**.

WE ARE TIRED OF BEING **BEATEN** BY POLICEMEN.

WE ARE TIRED OF SEEING OUR PEOPLE LOCKED UP IN JAIL **OVER** AND **OVER** AGAIN.

169

WE WILL MARCH THROUGH THE SOUTH; THROUGH THE STREETS OF **JACKSON**, THROUGH THE STREETS OF **DANVILLE**, THROUGH THE STREETS OF **CAMBRIDGE**, THROUGH THE STREETS OF **BIRMINGHAM**.

BUT WE WILL MARCH WITH THE SPIRIT OF **LOVE** AND WITH THE SPIRIT OF **DIGNITY** THAT WE HAVE SHOWN HERE **TODAY**.

BY THE FORCE OF OUR DEMANDS, OUR DETERMINATION, AND OUR NUMBERS, WE SHALL SPLINTER THE SEGREGATED SOUTH INTO A THOUSAND PIECES, AND PUT THEM TOGETHER IN THE IMAGE OF GOD AND DEMOCRACY.

WE MUST SAY: "WAKE UP, AMERICA!"

"WAKE UP!!

FOR WE CANNOT STOP,

AND WE **WILL NOT** AND **CANNOT** BE PATIENT.

DR. KING WAS THE DAY'S LAST SPEAKER.

HE STARTED SLOW. I'D HEARD HIM SPEAK
MANY TIMES. HIS CADENCE WAS SO FAMILIAR TO ME.

BUT AS HE FOUND HIS STRENGTH,
HIS **POWER**, HE TRANSFORMED THE
STEPS OF THE LINCOLN MEMORIAL
INTO A MODERN-DAY **PULPIT**.

HIS WORDS CARRIED THROUGH THE AIR
LIKE **ARROWS**... MOVING TO A CLIMACTIC
REFRAIN THE WORLD WOULD
NEVER FORGET.

TELL 'EM ABOUT
THE <u>DREAM</u>,
MARTIN.

IN THOSE MOMENTS, DR. KING MADE PLAIN ALL OF OUR HOPES, OUR ASPIRATIONS...

EVERYTHING WE SOUGHT THROUGH THE BEATINGS AND THE BLOOD, THROUGH THE TRIUMPHS AND FAILURES,

EVERYTHING WE DARED TO IMAGINE ABOUT A NEW AMERICA, A BETTER AMERICA,

IN WHICH EACH OF GOD'S CHILDREN CAN LIVE IN A SOCIETY THAT MAKES LOVE ITS HIGHEST VIRTUE.

JANUARY 20, 2009.

10:22 AM,
SUNDAY, SEPTEMBER 15, 1963.
YOUTH SUNDAY.
MINDFUL OF THE SACRIFICES BORNE BY OUR ANCESTORS.
TELEPHONE

SIXTEENTH STREET BAPTIST CHURCH--
BIRMINGHAM, AL.

ACKNOWLEDGMENTS

I am deeply grateful to Andrew Aydin for all of his hard work. He had a vision, and he never gave up. I believe together we have created something truly meaningful. I want to thank Nate Powell for his unbelievable talent, kind spirit, and hard work. He is a wonderful collaborator. And I want to thank Chris Staros, Brett Warnock, Leigh Walton, Chris Ross, and everyone at Top Shelf for their openness, their support, and their powerful work.

John Lewis

I want to thank my Mom for the opportunities in my life that her hard work and sacrifice made possible. I am forever indebted to John Lewis for his remarkable life, his trust, his faith, and his friendship. I am in awe of Nate Powell's talent and grateful to work with him. I want to thank Sara for her patience and support, Vaughn for his guidance and friendship, and Dom for reminding me to have fun. I wish Jordan could see this. And thank you Mr. Parker, Mrs. Fuentes, Jacob Gillison, A.D., Professor Uchimura and all of the teachers and mentors that gave me the courage to walk this road.

Andrew Aydin

I'd like to dedicate my work on this book to the memory of Sarah Kirsch (1970–2012), whose compassion, humanity, vision, and talent deeply shaped the direction of my life from my early teenage years; to my wife Rachel, a true original and cranky do-gooder committed to helping those who need a hand; and to our amazing daughter Harper, in hopes of her growing into a world more humane, more considerate, more loving—a world she and her entire generation will inherit. Let's make the world worth it.

Nate Powell

**Dedicated to the memory of
John Seigenthaler
July 27th, 1927–July 11th, 2014**

Original Draft of SNCC Chairman John Lewis' Speech to the March

WE MARCH TODAY FOR JOBS AND FREEDOM, BUT WE HAVE NOTHING TO BE PROUD OF, for hundreds and thousands of our brothers are not here. They have no money for their transportation, for they are receiving starvation wages, or no wages at all.

In good conscience, we cannot support wholeheartedly the administration's civil rights bill, for it is too little and too late. There's not one thing in the bill that will protect our people from police brutality.

This bill will not protect young children and old women from police dogs and fire hoses, for engaging in peaceful demonstrations: This bill will not protect the citizens in Danville, Virginia, who must live in constant fear in a police state. This bill will not protect the hundreds of people who have been arrested on trumped-up charges. What about the three young men in Americus, Georgia, who face the death penalty for engaging in peaceful protest?

The voting section of this bill will not help thousands of black citizens who want to vote. It will not help the citizens of Mississippi, of Alabama and Georgia, who are qualified to vote but lack a sixth-grade education. "ONE MAN, ONE VOTE" is the African cry. It is ours, too. It must be ours.

People have been forced to leave their homes because they dared to exercise their right to register to vote. What is there in this bill to ensure the equality of a maid who earns $5 a week in the home of a family whose income is $100,000 a year?

For the first time in one hundred years this nation is being awakened to the fact that segregation is evil and that it must be destroyed in all forms. Your presence today proves that you have been aroused to the point of action.

We are now involved in a serious revolution. This nation is still a place of cheap political leaders who build their careers on immoral compromises and ally themselves with open forms of political, economic and social exploitation. What political leader here can stand up and say, "My party is the party of principles?" The party of Kennedy is also the party of Eastland. The party of Javits is also the party of Goldwater. Where is *our* party?

In some parts of the South we work in the fields from sunup to sundown for $12 a week. In Albany, Georgia, nine of our leaders have been indicted not by Dixiecrats but by the federal government for peaceful protest. But what did the federal government do when Albany's deputy sheriff beat attorney C. B. King and left him half dead? What did the federal government do when local police officials kicked and assaulted the pregnant wife of Slater King, and she lost her baby?

It seems to me that the Albany indictment is part of a conspiracy on the part of the federal government and local politicians in the interest of expediency.

I want to know, which side is the federal government on?

The revolution is at hand, and we must free ourselves of the chains of political and economic slavery.

The nonviolent revolution is saying, "We will not wait for the courts to act, for we have been waiting for hundreds of years. We will not wait for the President, the Justice Department, nor Congress, but we will take matters into our own hands and create a source of power, outside of any national structure, that could and would assure us a victory."

To those who have said, "Be patient and wait," we must say that "patience" is a dirty and nasty word. We cannot be patient, we do not want to be free gradually. We want our freedom, and we want it *now*. We cannot depend on any political party, for both the Democrats and the Republicans have betrayed the basic principles of the Declaration of Independence.

We all recognize the fact that if any radical social, political and economic changes are to take place in our society, the people, the masses, must bring them about. In the struggle, we must seek more than civil rights; we must work for the community of love, peace and true brotherhood. Our minds, souls and hearts cannot rest until freedom and justice exist for *all people*.

The revolution is a serious one. Mr. Kennedy is trying to take the revolution out of the streets and put it into the courts. Listen, Mr. Kennedy. Listen, Mr. Congressman. Listen, fellow citizens. The black masses are on the march for jobs and freedom, and we must say to the politicians that there won't be a "cooling-off" period.

All of us must get in the revolution. Get in and stay in the streets of every city, every village and every hamlet of this nation until true freedom comes, until the revolution is complete. In the Delta of Mississippi, in southwest Georgia, in Alabama, Harlem, Chicago, Detroit, Philadelphia and all over this nation, the black masses are on the march!

We won't stop now. All of the forces of Eastland, Barnett, Wallace and Thurmond won't stop this revolution. The time will come when we will not confine our marching to Washington. We will march through the South, through the heart of Dixie, the way Sherman did. We shall pursue our own "scorched earth" policy and burn Jim Crow to the ground — nonviolently. We shall fragment the South into a thousand pieces and put them back together in the image of democracy. We will make the action of the past few months look petty. And I say to you, WAKE UP AMERICA!

We will not stop. If we do not get meaningful legislation out of this Congress, the time will come when we will not confine our marching to Washington. We will march through the South, through the streets of Jackson, through the streets of Danville, through the streets of Cambridge, through the streets of Birmingham. But we will march with the spirit of love and with the spirit of dignity that we have shown here today.

By the force of our demands, our determination and our numbers, we shall splinter the segregated South into a thousand pieces and put them back together in the image of God and democracy.

We must say, "Wake up, America. *Wake up!!!*" For we cannot stop, and we *will* not be patient.

ABOUT THE AUTHORS

JOHN LEWIS is the U.S. Representative for Georgia's fifth congressional district and an American icon widely known for his role in the civil rights movement.

Photo by Eric Etheridge

As a student at American Baptist Theological Seminary in 1959, Lewis organized sit-in demonstrations at segregated lunch counters in Nashville, Tennessee. In 1961, he volunteered to participate in the Freedom Rides, which challenged segregation at interstate bus terminals across the South. He was beaten severely by angry mobs and arrested by police for challenging the injustice of "Jim Crow" segregation in the South.

From 1963 to 1966, Lewis was Chairman of the Student Nonviolent Coordinating Committee (SNCC). As head of SNCC, Lewis became a nationally recognized figure, dubbed one of the "Big Six" leaders of the civil rights movement. At the age of 23, he was an architect of and a keynote speaker at the historic March on Washington in August 1963.

In 1964, John Lewis coordinated SNCC efforts to organize voter registration drives and community action programs during the Mississippi Freedom Summer. The following year, Lewis helped spearhead one of the most seminal moments of the civil rights movement. Together with Hosea Williams, another notable civil rights leader, John Lewis led over 600 peaceful, orderly protesters across the Edmund Pettus Bridge in Selma, Alabama, on March 7, 1965. They intended to march from Selma to Montgomery to demonstrate the need for voting rights in the state. The marchers were attacked by Alabama state troopers in a brutal confrontation that became known as "Bloody Sunday." News broadcasts and photographs revealing the senseless cruelty of the segregated South helped hasten the passage of the Voting Rights Act of 1965.

Despite physical attacks, serious injuries, and more than 40 arrests, John Lewis remained a devoted advocate of the philosophy of nonviolence. After leaving SNCC in 1966, he continued to work for civil rights, first as Associate Director of the Field Foundation, then with the Southern Regional Council, where he became Executive Director of the Voter Education Project (VEP). In 1977, Lewis was appointed by President Jimmy Carter to direct more than 250,000 volunteers of ACTION, the federal volunteer agency.

In 1981, Lewis was elected to the Atlanta City Council. He was elected to the U.S. House of Representatives in November 1986 and has represented Georgia's fifth district there ever since. In 2011 he was awarded the Medal of Freedom by President Barack Obama.

Lewis's 1998 memoir, *Walking with the Wind: A Memoir of the Movement*, won numerous honors, including the Robert F. Kennedy, Lillian Smith, and Anisfield-Wolf Book Awards. His subsequent book, *Across That Bridge: Life Lessons and a Vision for Change*, won the NAACP Image Award.

(From left to right): Nate Powell, Congressman John Lewis, Andrew Aydin.

Photo by Sandi Villarreal

ANDREW AYDIN, an Atlanta native, currently serves as Digital Director & Policy Advisor in the Washington, D.C., office of Rep. John Lewis. After learning that his boss had been inspired as a young man by the 1950s comic book *Martin Luther King & The Montgomery Story*, Aydin conceived the *March* series and collaborated with Rep. Lewis to write it, while also composing a master's thesis on the history and impact of *The Montgomery Story*. Today, he continues to write comics and lecture about the history of comics in the civil rights movement.

Previously, he served as Communications Director and Press Secretary during Rep. Lewis's 2008 and 2010 re-election campaigns, as District Aide to Rep. John Larson (D-CT), and as Special Assistant to Connecticut Lt. Governor Kevin Sullivan. Aydin is a graduate of the Lovett School in Atlanta, Trinity College in Hartford, and Georgetown University in Washington, D.C. Visit www.andrewaydin.com for more information.

NATE POWELL is a *New York Times* best-selling graphic novelist born in Little Rock, Arkansas, in 1978. He began self-publishing at age 14, and graduated from School of Visual Arts in 2000.

His work includes *You Don't Say, Any Empire, Swallow Me Whole, The Silence of Our Friends, The Year of the Beasts*, and Rick Riordan's *The Lost Hero*. Powell's comics have received such honors as the Eisner Award, two Ignatz Awards, four YALSA Great Graphic Novels for Teens selections, and a *Los Angeles Times* Book Prize finalist selection.

In addition to *March*, Powell has spoken about his work at the United Nations and created animated illustrations for SPLC's documentary *Selma: The Bridge to the Ballot*.

Powell is currently writing and drawing his next book, *Cover*, and drawing *Two Dead* with writer Van Jansen. He lives in Bloomington, Indiana. Visit Nate's website at www.seemybrotherdance.org for more information.

PRAISE FOR THE *MARCH* TRILOGY

March: Book One
128 pages, $14.95 (US)
ISBN: 978-1-60309-300-2

March: Book Two
192 pages, $19.95 (US)
ISBN: 978-1-60309-400-9

March: Book Three
256 pages, $19.99 (US)
ISBN: 978-1-60309-402-3

March (Trilogy Slipcase Set)
Three Volumes, $49.99 (US)
ISBN: 978-1-60309-395-8

#1 *New York Times* and *Washington Post* Bestseller
National Book Award
Will Eisner Comic Industry Award
Coretta Scott King Book Award—Author Honor
Robert F. Kennedy Book Award—Special Recognition
Street Literature Book Award Medal
ALA Notable Books
YALSA's Top 10 Great Graphic Novels for Teens
YALSA's Outstanding Books for the College Bound
***Reader's Digest*'s Graphic Novels Every Grown-Up Should Read**
Added to New York City Schools curriculum and taught in over 40 states
Selected for college & university reading programs across America

"Congressman John Lewis has been a resounding moral voice in the quest for equality for more than 50 years, and I'm so pleased that he is sharing his memories of the Civil Rights Movement with America's young leaders. In *March*, he brings a whole new generation with him across the Edmund Pettus Bridge, from a past of clenched fists into a future of outstretched hands."
—President Bill Clinton

"With *March*, Congressman John Lewis takes us behind the scenes of some of the most pivotal moments of the Civil Rights Movement. In graphic novel form, his first-hand account makes these historic events both accessible and relevant to an entire new generation of Americans."
— LeVar Burton

"*March* is one of the most important graphic novels ever created—an extraordinary presentation of an extraordinary life, and proof that young people can change the world. I'm stunned by the power of these comics, and grateful that Congressman Lewis's story will enlighten and inspire future generations of readers and leaders."
— Raina Telgemeier

"There is perhaps no more important modern book to be stocked in American school libraries than *March*."
— *The Washington Post*

"Essential reading…*March* is a moving and important achievement…the story of a true American superhero."
—*USA Today*

"Emphasizing disruption, decentralization and cooperation over the mythic ascent of heroic leaders, this graphic novel's presentation of civil rights is startlingly contemporary."

— *The New York Times*

"Superbly told history." —*Publishers Weekly* (starred review)

"Powell captures the danger and tension in stunning cinematic spreads, which dramatically complement Lewis's powerful story…The story of the civil rights movement is a triumphant one, but Lewis's account is full of nuance and personal struggle, both of which impart an empowering human element to an often mythologized period of history…this is a must-read."

— *Booklist* (starred review)

"An astonishingly accomplished graphic memoir that brings to life a vivid portrait of the civil rights era, Lewis's extraordinary history and accomplishments, and the movement he helped lead…Its power, accessibility and artistry destine it for awards, and a well-deserved place at the pinnacle of the comics canon." —NPR

"*March* provides a potent reminder that the sit-ins, far from being casually assembled, were well-coordinated, disciplined events informed by a rigorous philosophy…Likely to prove inspirational to readers for years to come." —*Barnes and Noble Review*

"A riveting chronicle of Lewis's extraordinary life…it powerfully illustrates how much perseverance is needed to achieve fundamental social change." —*O, The Oprah Magazine*

"*March* offers a poignant portrait of an iconic figure that both entertains and edifies, and deserves to be placed alongside other historical graphic memoirs like *Persepolis* and *Maus*."

—*Entertainment Weekly*

"The civil rights movement can seem to some like a distant memory…John Lewis refreshes our memories in dramatic fashion." —*The Chicago Tribune*

"When a graphic novel tries to interest young readers in an important topic, it often feels forced. Not so with the exhilarating *March*…Powerful words and pictures." —*The Boston Globe*

"This memoir puts a human face on a struggle that many students will primarily know from textbooks… Visually stunning, the black-and-white illustrations convey the emotions of this turbulent time…This insider's view of the civil rights movement should be required reading for young and old; not to be missed." —*School Library Journal* (starred review)

"A powerful tale of courage and principle igniting sweeping social change, told by a strong-minded, uniquely qualified eyewitness…The heroism of those who sat and marched…comes through with vivid, inspiring clarity." —*Kirkus Reviews* (starred review)

"Lewis's remarkable life has been skillfully translated into graphics…Segregation's insult to personhood comes across here with a visual, visceral punch. This version of Lewis's life story belongs in libraries to teach readers about the heroes of America."

—*Library Journal* (starred review)

"Powell's drawings in *March* combine the epic sweep of history with the intimate personal details of memoir, and bring Lewis's story to life in a way that feels entirely unfamiliar. *March* is shaping up to be a major work of history and graphic literature." —*Slate*

"In a new graphic memoir, the civil rights leader shows youth how to get in trouble— good trouble." —*In These Times*

March: Book Two © 2015 John Lewis and Andrew Aydin.

Written by John Lewis and Andrew Aydin
Art by Nate Powell

Published by Top Shelf Productions
PO Box 1282
Marietta, GA 30061-1282
USA

Editor-in-Chief: Chris Staros

Edited by Leigh Walton
Designed by Chris Ross and Nate Powell
Cover Coloring on Three-Volume Slipcase Edition: José Villarrubia

Publicity by Leigh Walton (leigh@topshelfcomix.com)

Visit our online catalog at www.topshelfcomix.com.

Printed in Korea.

2023   2022   2021   2020   11   12   13   14